MAJESTIC EXPRESSIONS
Relax, Refresh, Renew

COLORING JOURNAL

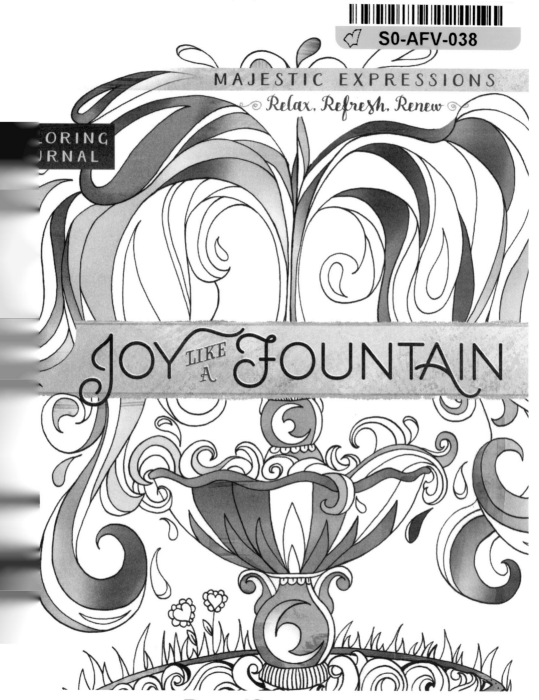

JOY LIKE A FOUNTAIN

BroadStreet
P U B L I S H I N G

BroadStreet Publishing Group LLC
Racine, Wisconsin, USA
Broadstreetpublishing.com

MAJESTIC EXPRESSIONS

JOY LIKE A FOUNTAIN

© 2016 by BroadStreet Publishing

ISBN 978-1-4245-5166-8

Cover design by Chris Garborg | garborgdesign.com
Compiled and edited by Michelle Winger | literallyprecise.com

Printed in the United States of America.

16 17 18 19 20 21 22   7 6 5 4 3 2 1

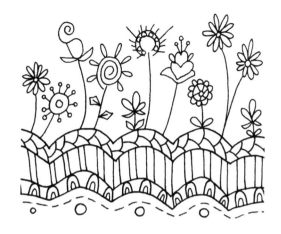

INTRODUCTION

There is plenty of research that shows coloring to be an effective stress reducer. Maybe you picked up this book because you've heard the hype and you're curious. Maybe you love to write. If you've been looking for a way to relax and express your creativity at the same time, here it is! Every time you open this coloring journal, you enter a stress-free zone.

While this is a great distraction from all you have going on, the best way to find lasting peace is to spend time with your Creator. As you fill the intricately designed illustrations and empty lines with your unique style of expression, dwell on the richness of God's Word, the faithfulness of his character, and the depth of his love for you.

BE INSPIRED!

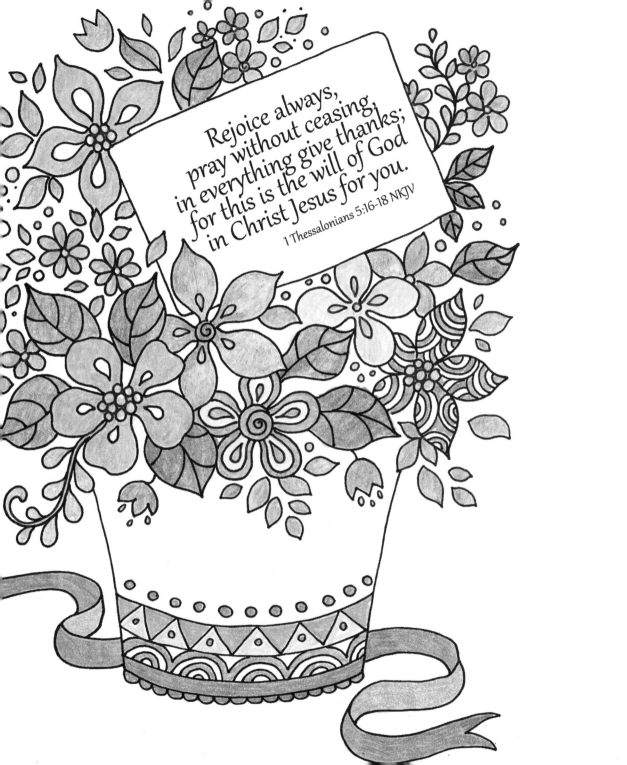

Rejoice always,
pray without ceasing,
in everything give thanks;
for this is the will of God
in Christ Jesus for you.

1 Thessalonians 5:16-18 NKJV

YOU HAVE GRANTED HIM UNENDING BLESSINGS
AND MADE HIM GLAD WITH THE JOY OF YOUR PRESENCE.

PSALM 21:6 NIV

_____

_____

_____

_____

_____

_____

_____

_____

_____

_____

_____

_____

_____

_____

_____

_____

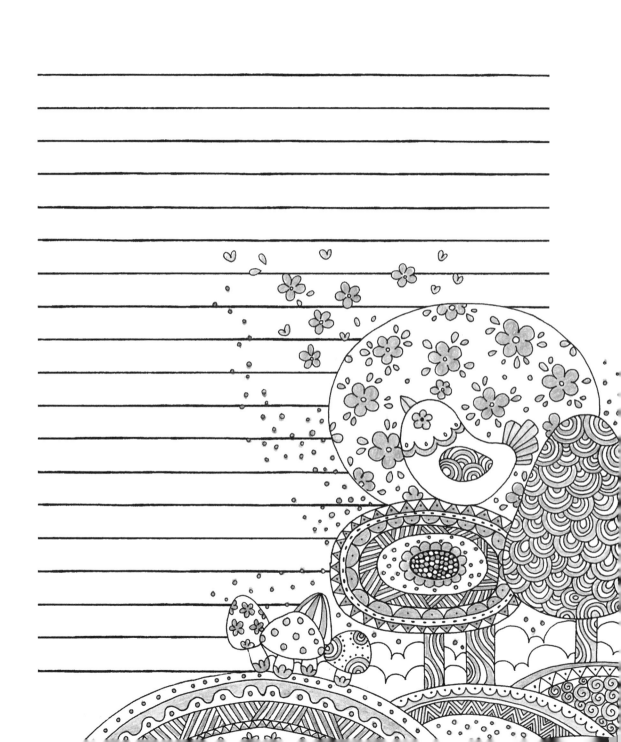

_____

_____

_____

_____

_____

_____

_____

_____

_____

_____

_____

_____

_____

_____

_____

_____

_____

_____

THE LORD YOUR GOD WILL BLESS YOU IN ALL YOUR HARVEST AND IN ALL
THE WORK OF YOUR HANDS, AND YOUR JOY WILL BE COMPLETE.

DEUTERONOMY 16:15 NIV

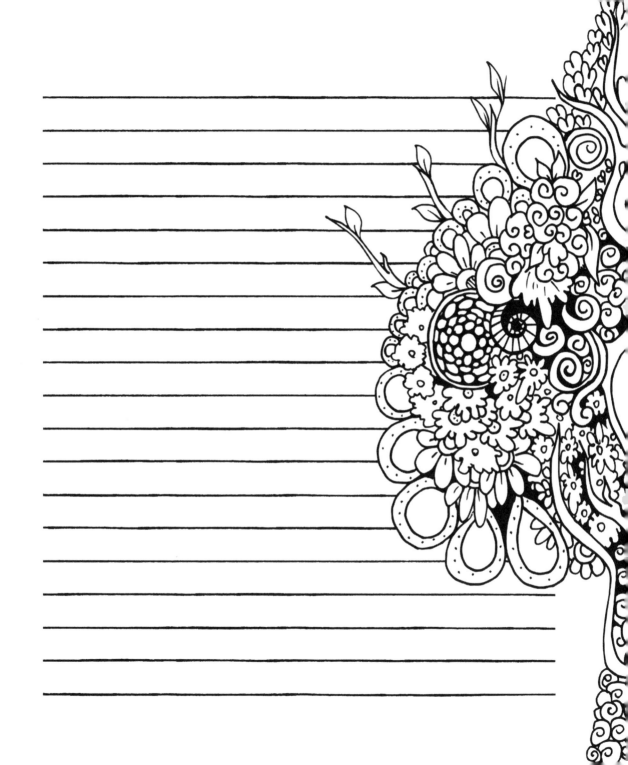

HE BROUGHT HIS PEOPLE OUT WITH JOY, HIS CHOSEN ONES WITH SINGING.

PSALM 105:43 ESV

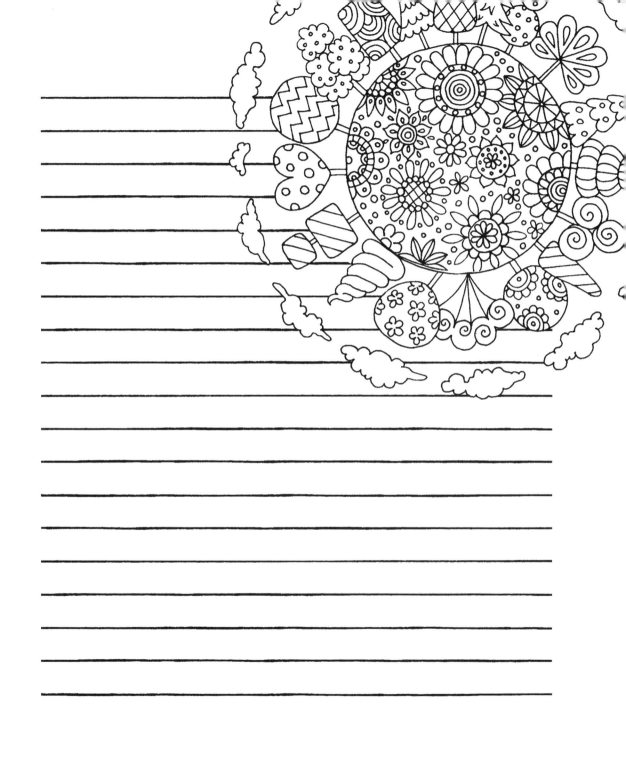

_____

_____

_____

_____

_____

_____

_____

_____

_____

_____

_____

_____

_____

_____

_____

_____

LET THE GODLY REJOICE. LET THEM BE GLAD IN GOD'S PRESENCE.
LET THEM BE FILLED WITH JOY.

PSALM 68:3 NLT

THOSE WHO SOW IN TEARS SHALL REAP IN JOY.

PSALM 126:5 NKJV

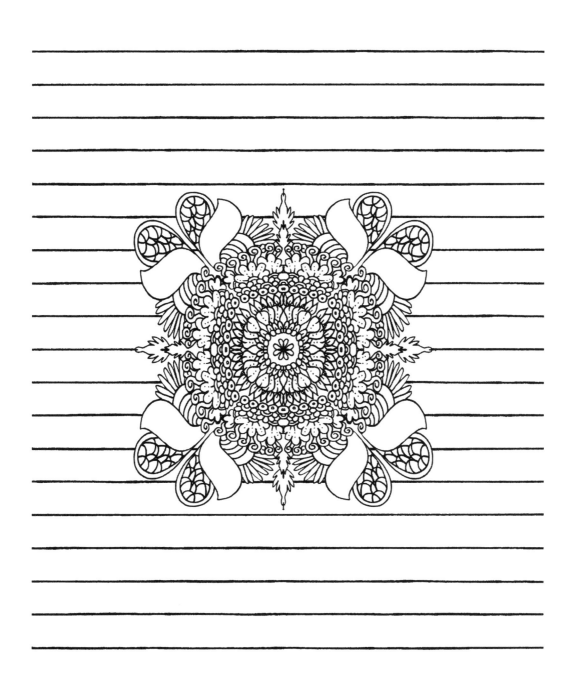

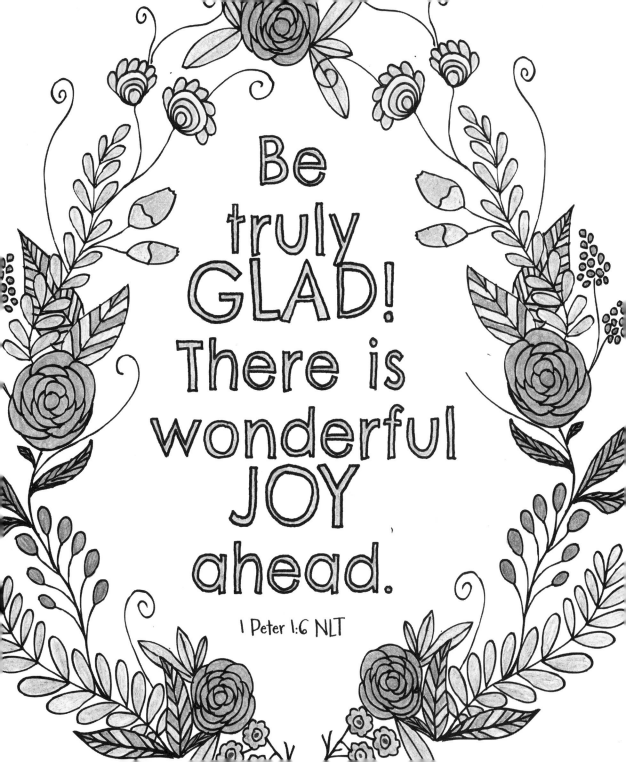

Be truly GLAD! There is wonderful JOY ahead.

1 Peter 1:6 NLT

CONSIDER IT PURE JOY, MY BROTHERS AND SISTERS,
WHENEVER YOU FACE TRIALS OF MANY KINDS, BECAUSE YOU KNOW
THAT THE TESTING OF YOUR FAITH PRODUCES PERSEVERANCE.

JAMES 1:2-3 NIV

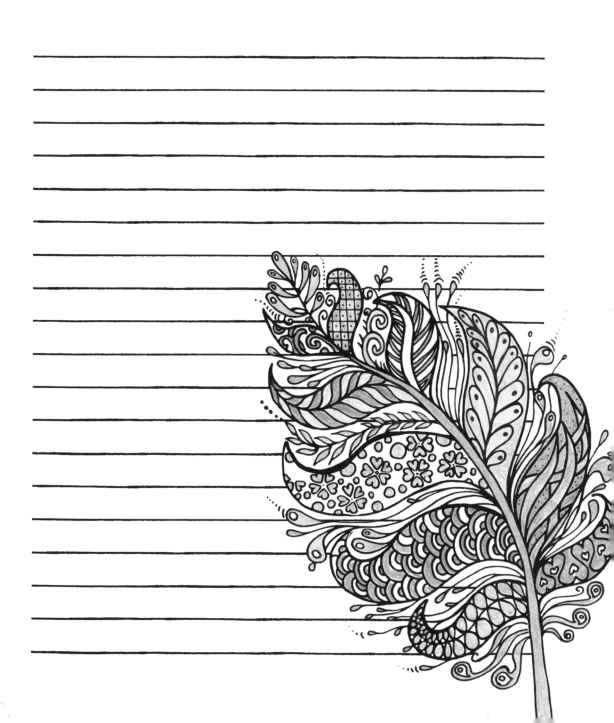

A PERSON FINDS JOY IN GIVING AN APT REPLY—
AND HOW GOOD IS A TIMELY WORD!

PROVERBS 15:23 NIV

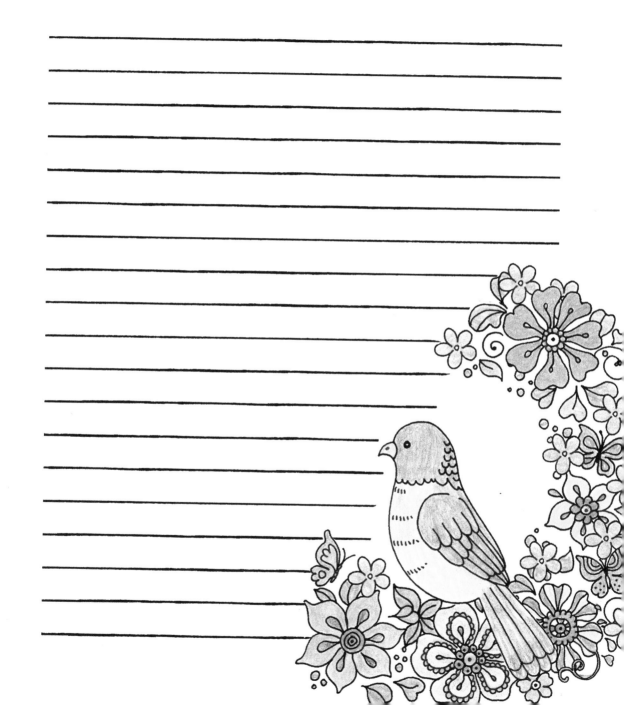

COME, EVERYONE! CLAP YOUR HANDS! SHOUT TO GOD WITH JOYFUL PRAISE!
PSALM 47:1 NLT

_____

_____

_____

_____

_____

_____

_____

_____

_____

_____

_____

_____

_____

_____

_____

_____

_____

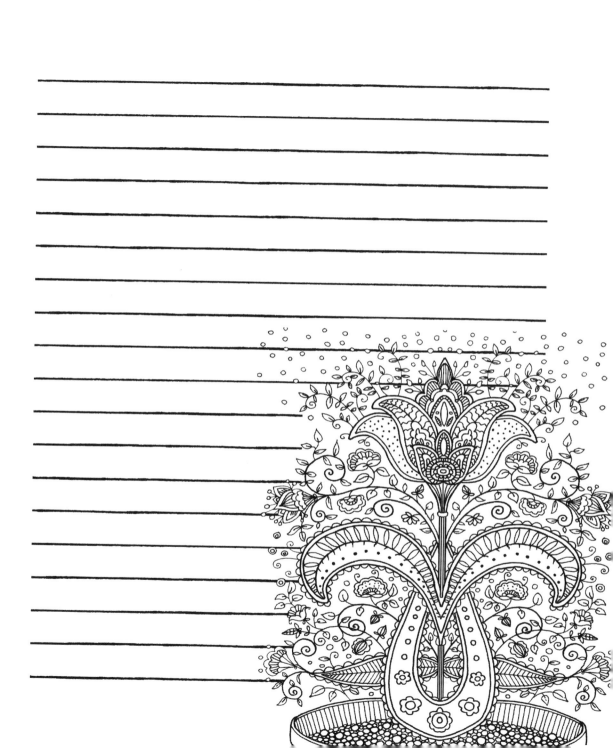

_____

_____

_____

_____

_____

_____

_____

_____

_____

_____

_____

_____

_____

_____

THEY WILL ENTER ZION WITH SINGING; EVERLASTING
JOY WILL CROWN THEIR HEADS. GLADNESS AND JOY WILL OVERTAKE THEM,
AND SORROW AND SIGHING WILL FLEE AWAY.

ISAIAH 51:11 NIV

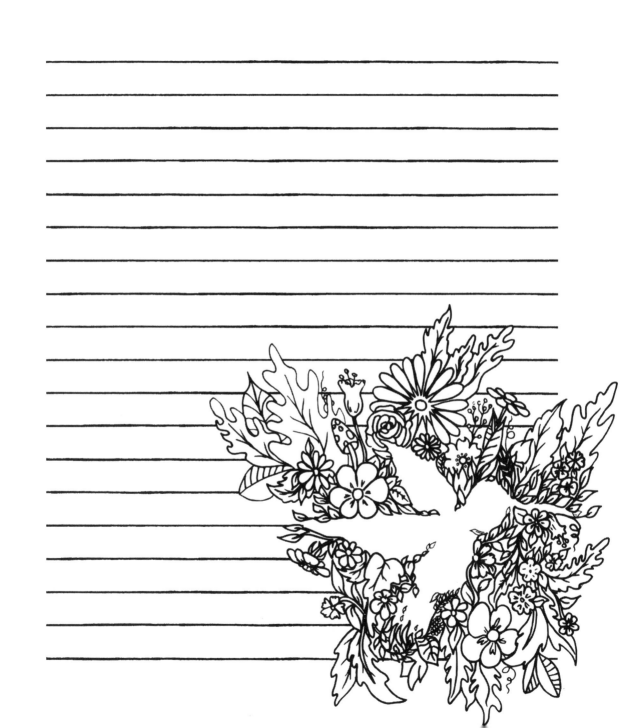

_____

_____

_____

_____

_____

_____

_____

_____

_____

_____

_____

_____

_____

_____

_____

_____

_____

_____

_____

_____

YOU WILL SHOW ME THE PATH OF LIFE; IN YOUR PRESENCE IS FULLNESS OF
JOY; AT YOUR RIGHT HAND ARE PLEASURES FOREVERMORE.

PSALM 16:11 NKJV

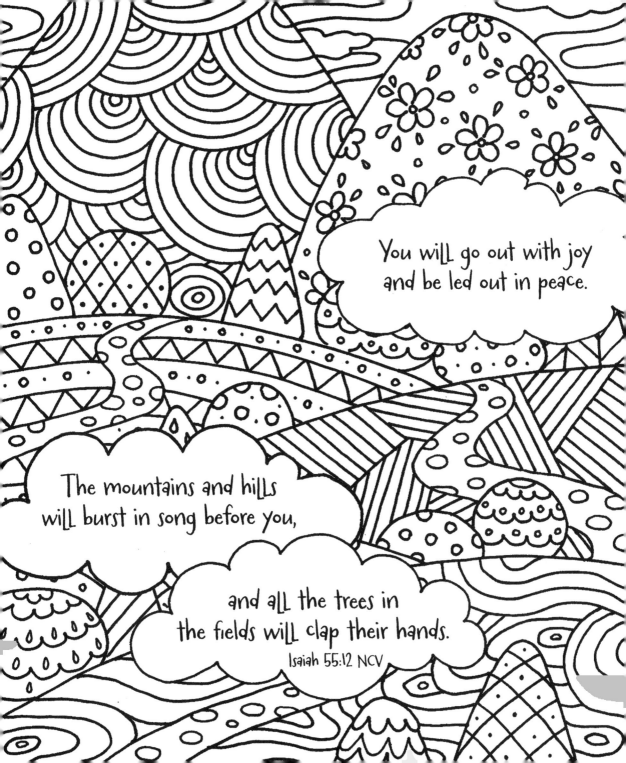

THE HUMBLE WILL BE FILLED WITH FRESH JOY FROM THE LORD.

ISAIAH 29:19 NLT

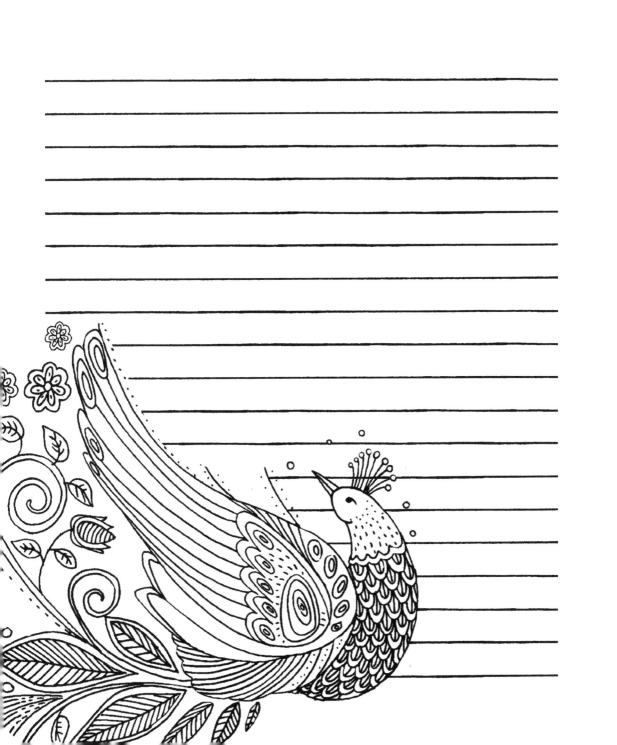

_____

_____

_____

_____

_____

_____

_____

_____

_____

_____

_____

_____

_____

_____

FOR THE KINGDOM OF GOD IS NOT A MATTER OF WHAT WE EAT OR DRINK,
BUT OF LIVING A LIFE OF GOODNESS AND PEACE
AND JOY IN THE HOLY SPIRIT.

ROMANS 14:17 NLT

_____

_____

_____

_____

_____

_____

_____

_____

_____

_____

_____

_____

_____

_____

_____

_____

LET THE FIELDS AND THEIR CROPS BURST OUT WITH JOY!
LET THE TREES OF THE FOREST RUSTLE WITH PRAISE.

PSALM 96:12 NLT

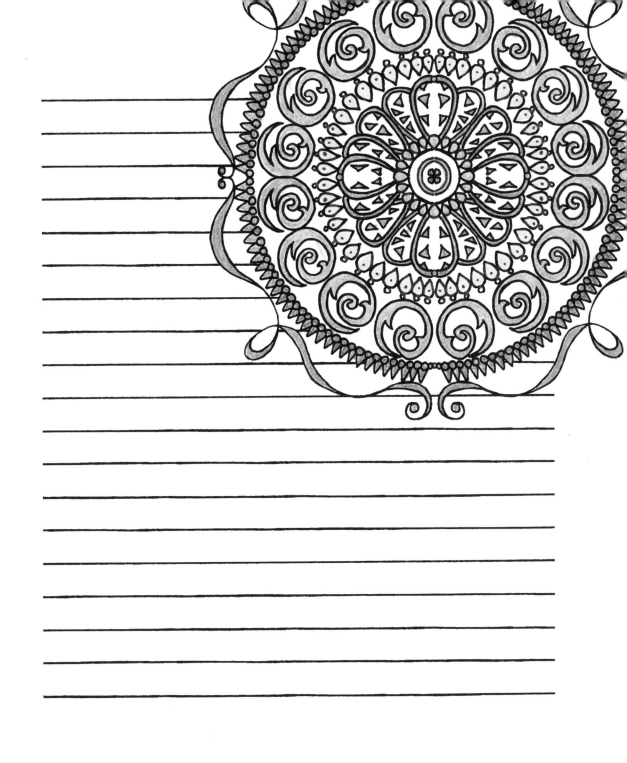

YOU HAVE BEEN MY HELP, AND IN THE SHADOW OF
YOUR WINGS I SING FOR JOY.
PSALM 63:7 NASB

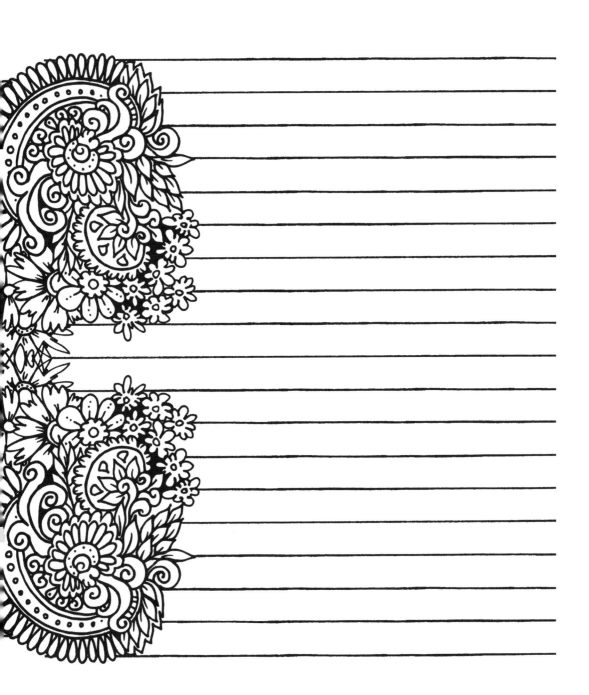

_____

_____

_____

_____

_____

_____

_____

_____

_____

_____

_____

_____

_____

_____

_____

_____

_____

_____

I WILL TURN THEIR MOURNING INTO JOY; I WILL COMFORT THEM,
AND GIVE THEM GLADNESS FOR SORROW.

JEREMIAH 31:13 ESV

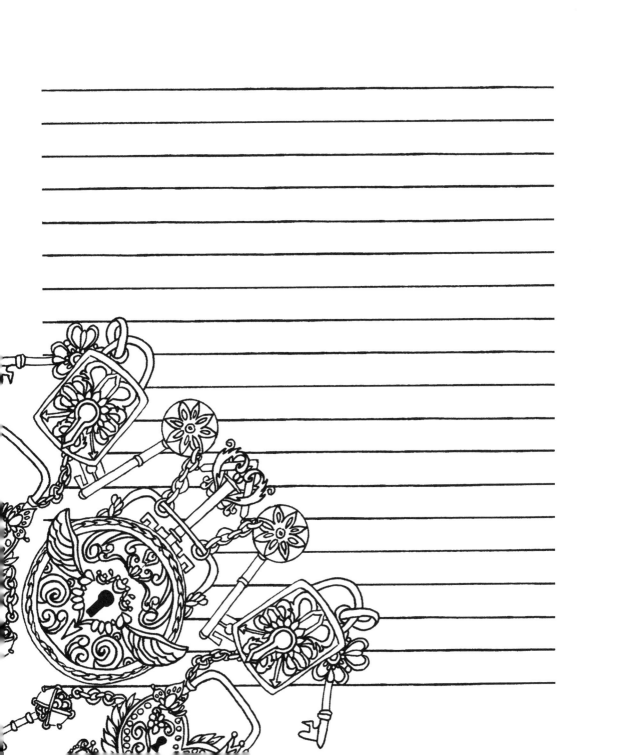

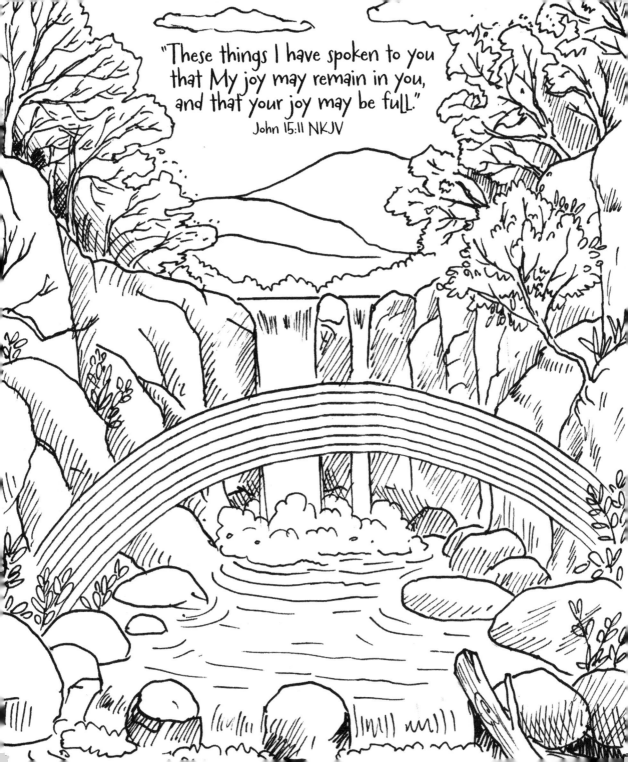

"These things I have spoken to you that My joy may remain in you, and that your joy may be full."

John 15:11 NKJV

FOR THE JOY SET BEFORE HIM HE ENDURED THE CROSS, SCORNING ITS SHAME, AND SAT DOWN AT THE RIGHT HAND OF THE THRONE OF GOD.

HEBREWS 12:2 NIV

_____

_____

_____

_____

_____

_____

_____

_____

_____

_____

_____

_____

_____

_____

THOUGH YOU HAVE NOT SEEN HIM, YOU LOVE HIM;
AND EVEN THOUGH YOU DO NOT SEE HIM NOW, YOU BELIEVE IN HIM
AND ARE FILLED WITH AN INEXPRESSIBLE AND GLORIOUS JOY.

1 PETER 1:8 NIV

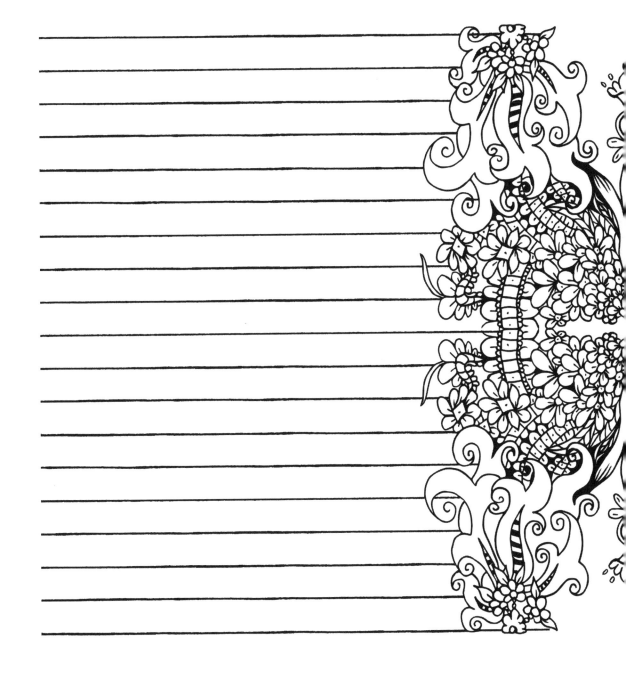

YOU HAVE SORROW NOW, BUT I WILL SEE YOU AGAIN;
THEN YOU WILL REJOICE, AND NO ONE CAN ROB YOU OF THAT JOY.
JOHN 16:22 NLT

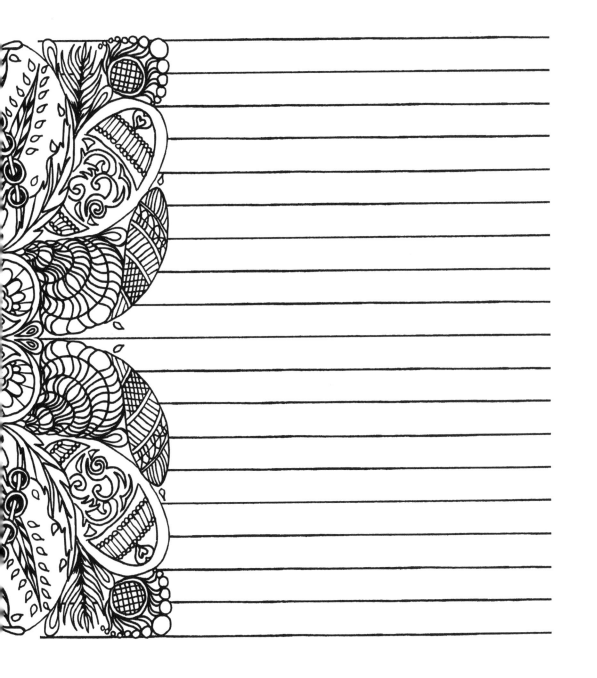

_____

_____

_____

_____

_____

_____

_____

_____

_____

_____

_____

_____

_____

_____

_____

_____

LET THE HEAVENS BE GLAD, AND THE EARTH REJOICE!
LET THE SEA AND EVERYTHING IN IT SHOUT HIS PRAISE!

PSALM 96:11 NLT

A JOYFUL HEART IS GOOD MEDICINE.

PROVERBS 17:22 ESV

_____

_____

_____

_____

_____

_____

_____

_____

_____

_____

_____

_____

_____

_____

_____

_____

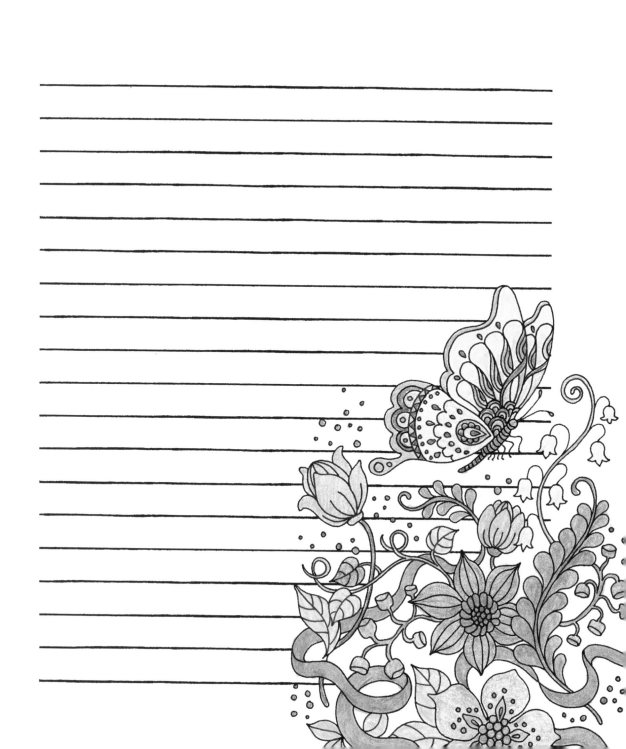

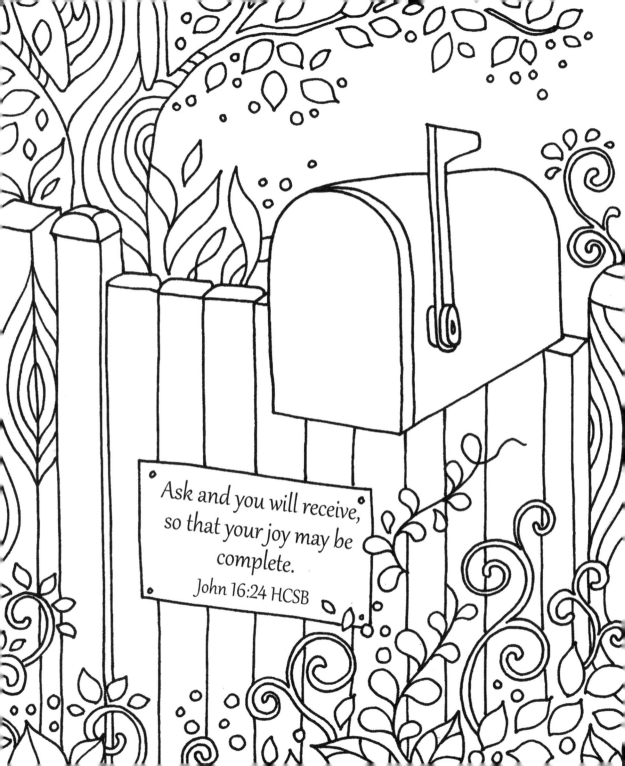

Ask and you will receive, so that your joy may be complete.

John 16:24 HCSB

I COMMEND THE ENJOYMENT OF LIFE, BECAUSE THERE IS NOTHING BETTER FOR A PERSON UNDER THE SUN THAN TO EAT AND DRINK AND BE GLAD. THEN JOY WILL ACCOMPANY THEM IN THEIR TOIL ALL THE DAYS OF THE LIFE GOD HAS GIVEN THEM UNDER THE SUN.

ECCLESIASTES 8:15 NIV

_____

_____

_____

_____

_____

_____

_____

_____

_____

_____

_____

_____

_____

_____

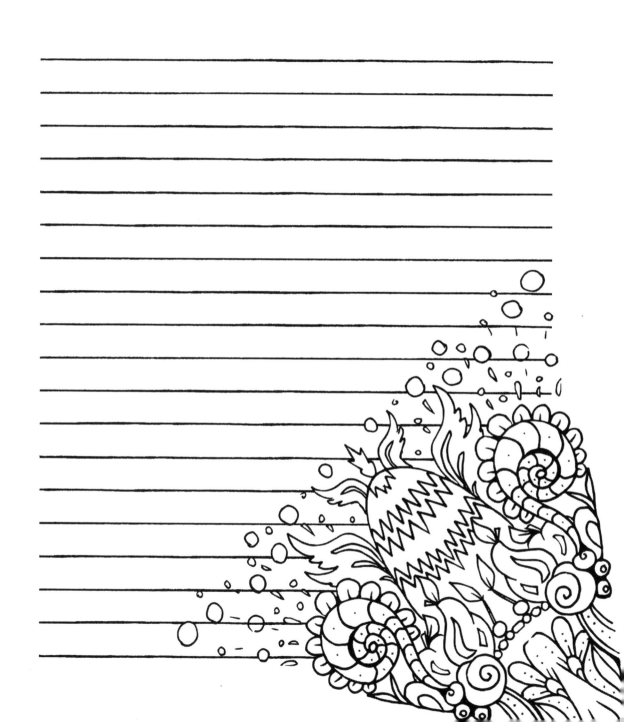

BE TRULY GLAD. THERE IS WONDERFUL JOY AHEAD.

1 PETER 1:6 NLT

LET ALL WHO TAKE REFUGE IN YOU REJOICE;
LET THEM SHOUT FOR JOY FOREVER. MAY YOU SHELTER THEM,
AND MAY THOSE WHO LOVE YOUR NAME BOAST ABOUT YOU.
PSALM 5:11 HCSB

THE EXERCISE OF JUSTICE IS JOY FOR THE RIGHTEOUS.

PROVERBS 21:15 NASB

_____

_____

_____

_____

_____

_____

_____

_____

_____

_____

_____

_____

_____

_____

_____

_____

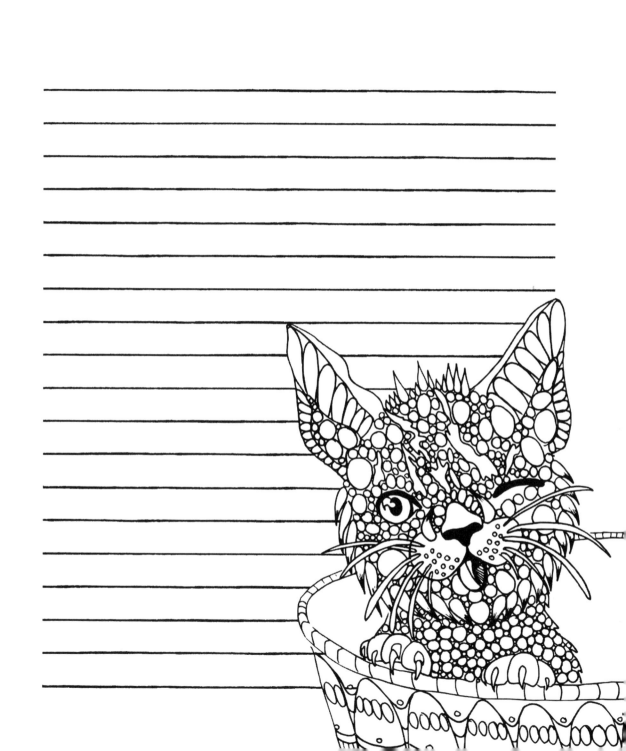

_____

_____

_____

_____

_____

_____

_____

_____

_____

_____

_____

_____

_____

_____

MAKE ME TRULY HAPPY BY AGREEING WHOLEHEARTEDLY
WITH EACH OTHER, LOVING ONE ANOTHER, AND WORKING TOGETHER
WITH ONE MIND AND PURPOSE.

PHILIPPIANS 2:2 NLT

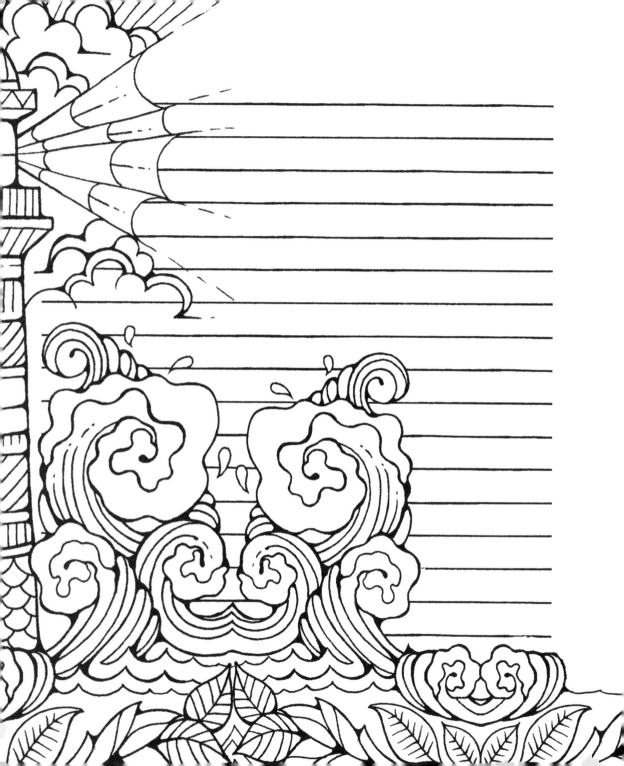

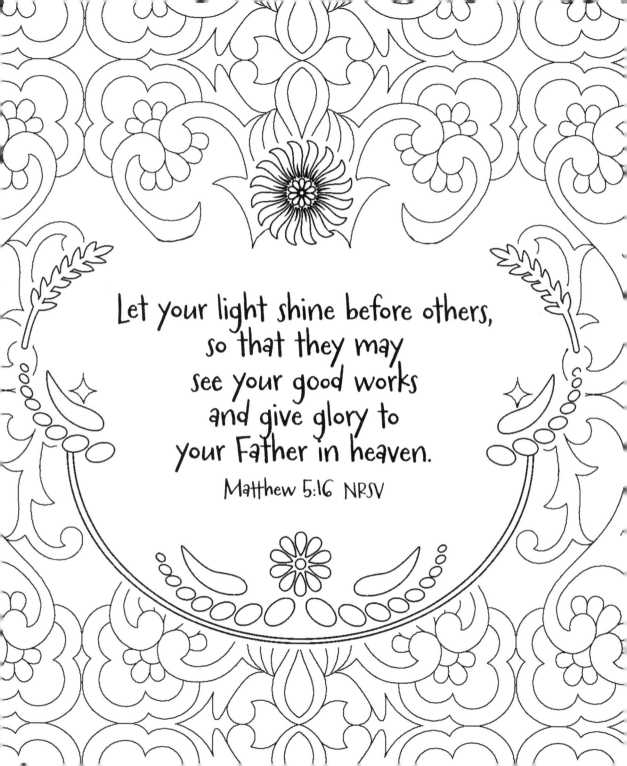

Let your light shine before others,
so that they may
see your good works
and give glory to
your Father in heaven.

Matthew 5:16 NRSV

_____

_____

_____

_____

_____

_____

_____

_____

_____

_____

_____

_____

_____

_____

_____

YOU HAVE PUT MORE JOY IN MY HEART
THAN THEY HAVE WHEN THEIR GRAIN AND NEW WINE ABOUND.

PSALM 4:7 HCSB

RESTORE TO ME THE JOY OF YOUR SALVATION
AND GRANT ME A WILLING SPIRIT, TO SUSTAIN ME.
PSALM 51:12 NIV

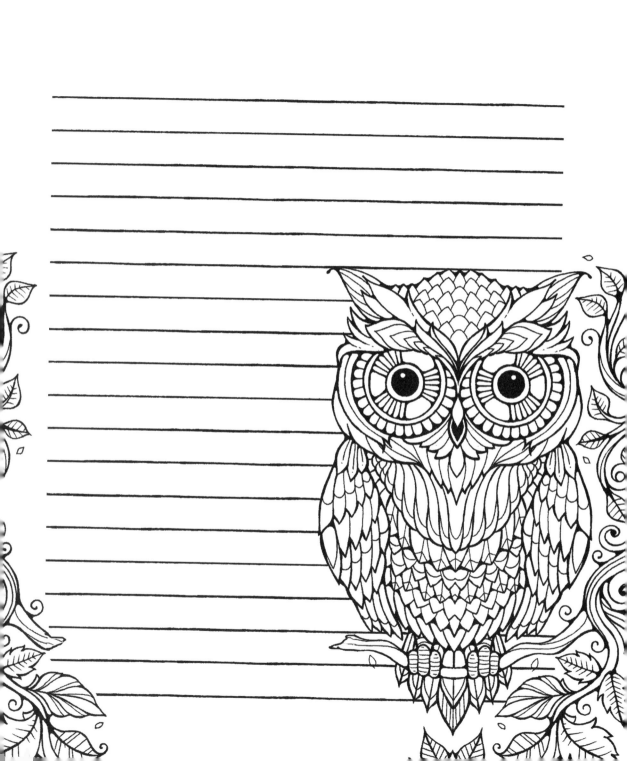

REJOICE IN THAT DAY AND LEAP FOR JOY,
BECAUSE GREAT IS YOUR REWARD IN HEAVEN.

LUKE 6:23 NIV

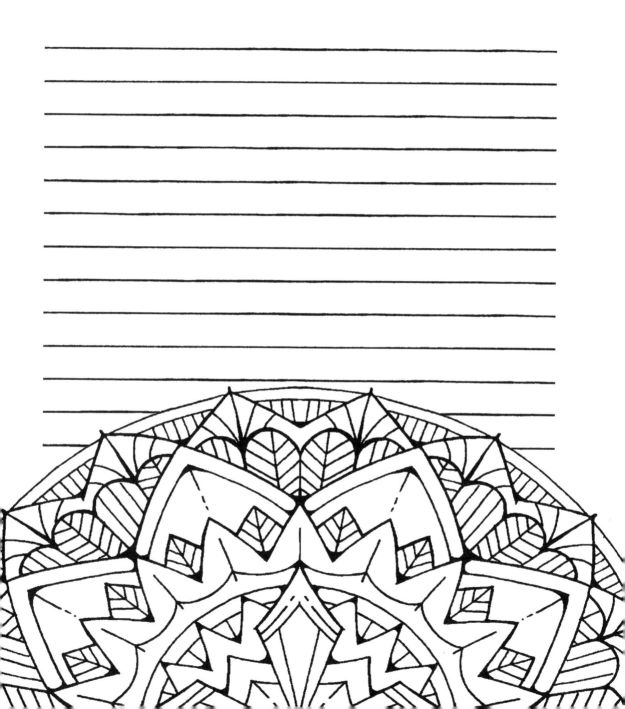

HIS ANGER LASTS ONLY A MOMENT, BUT HIS FAVOR, A LIFETIME. WEEPING
MAY SPEND THE NIGHT, BUT THERE IS JOY IN THE MORNING.
PSALM 30:5 HCSB

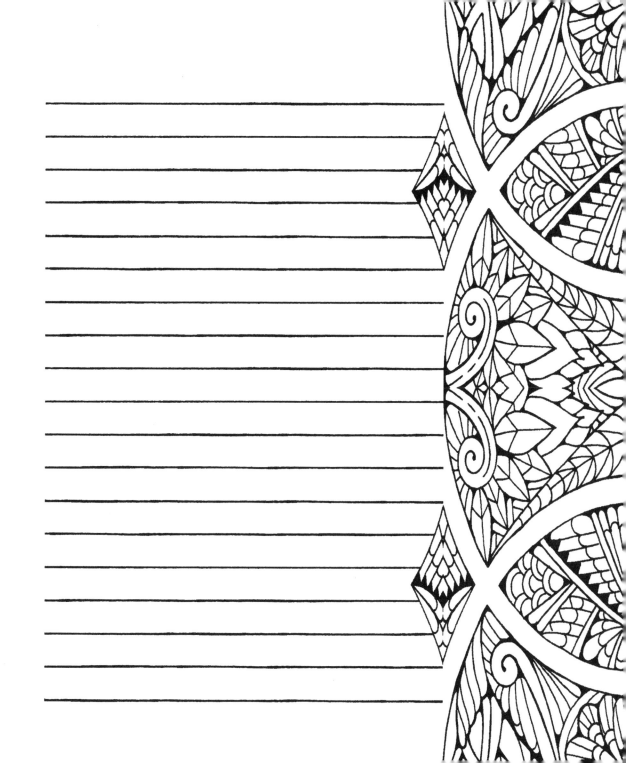

_____

_____

_____

_____

_____

_____

_____

_____

_____

_____

_____

_____

_____

_____

_____

_____

OUR MOUTHS WERE FILLED WITH LAUGHTER,
OUR TONGUES WITH SONGS OF JOY. THEN IT WAS SAID AMONG THE NATIONS,
"THE LORD HAS DONE GREAT THINGS FOR THEM."

PSALM 126:2 NIV

Whatever is TRUE, Whatever is NOBLE, Whatever is RIGHT, Whatever is PURE, Whatever is LOVELY, Whatever is ADMIRABLE - If Anything is EXCELLENT or PRAISEWORTHY - think about SUCH THINGS

PHILIPPIANS 4:8 NIV

_____

_____

_____

_____

_____

_____

_____

_____

_____

_____

_____

_____

_____

_____

_____

_____

REJOICE WITH THOSE WHO REJOICE.

ROMANS 12:15 NIV

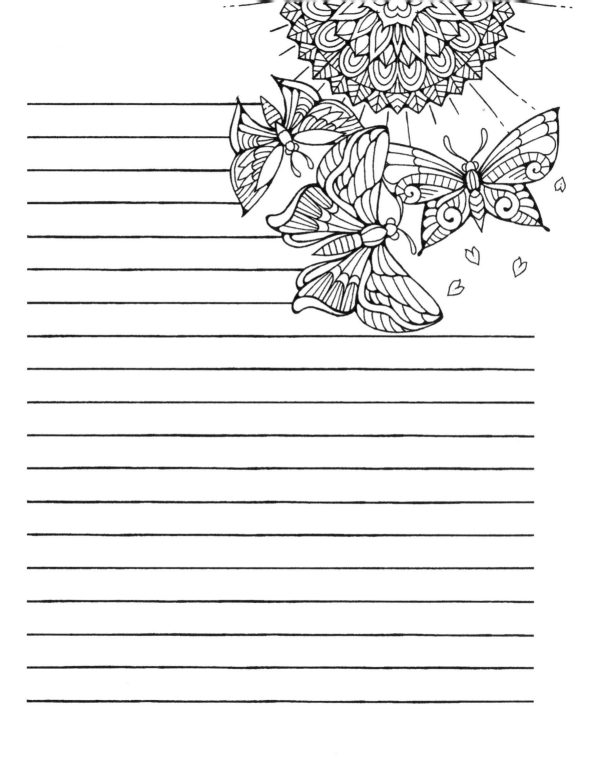

HAPPY ARE THOSE WHO HEAR THE JOYFUL CALL TO WORSHIP,
FOR THEY WILL WALK IN THE LIGHT OF YOUR PRESENCE, LORD.

PSALM 89:15 NLT

_____

_____

_____

_____

_____

_____

_____

_____

_____

_____

_____

_____

_____

_____

_____

_____

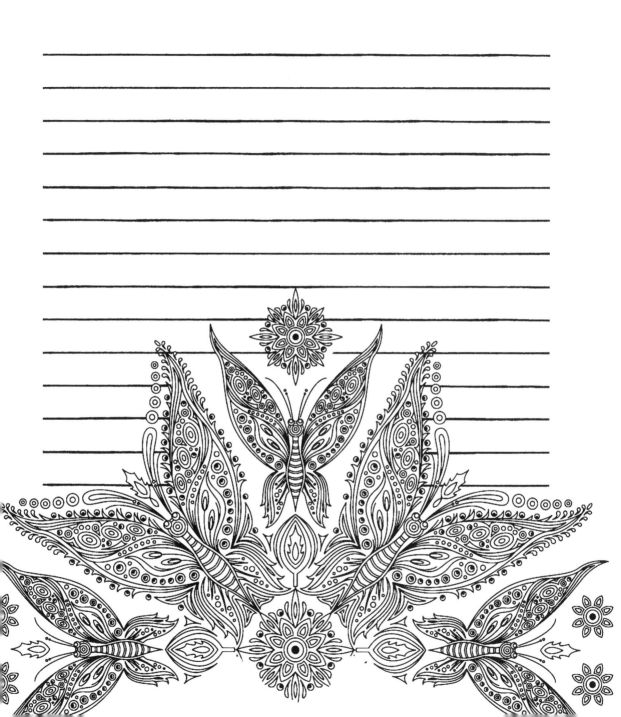

MAY YOU BE FILLED WITH JOY, ALWAYS THANKING THE FATHER.
HE HAS ENABLED YOU TO SHARE IN THE INHERITANCE THAT BELONGS
TO HIS PEOPLE, WHO LIVE IN THE LIGHT.

COLOSSIANS 1:11-12 NLT

_____

_____

_____

_____

_____

_____

_____

_____

_____

_____

_____

_____

_____

_____

_____

HE WILL YET FILL YOUR MOUTH WITH LAUGHTER
AND YOUR LIPS WITH SHOUTS OF JOY.

JOB 8:21 NIV

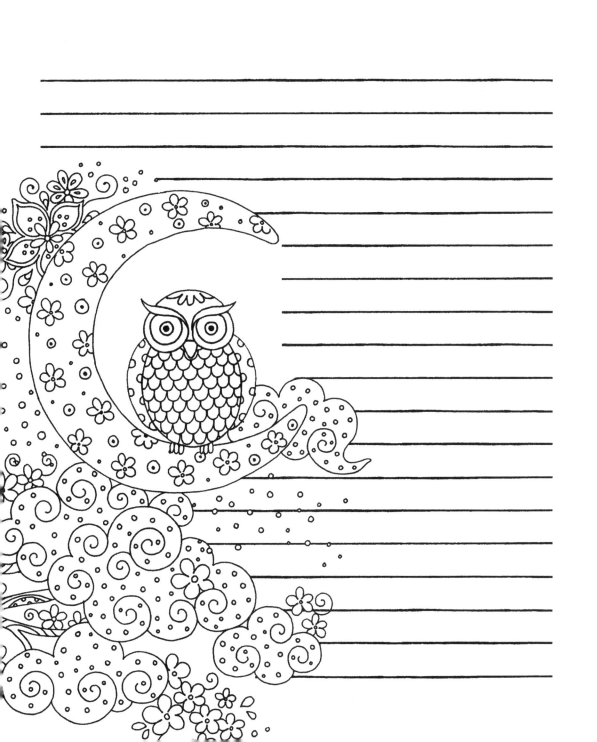

THE LORD HAS DONE GREAT THINGS FOR US, AND WE ARE FILLED WITH JOY.

PSALM 126:3 NIV

_____

_____

_____

_____

_____

_____

_____

_____

_____

_____

_____

_____

_____

_____

_____

_____

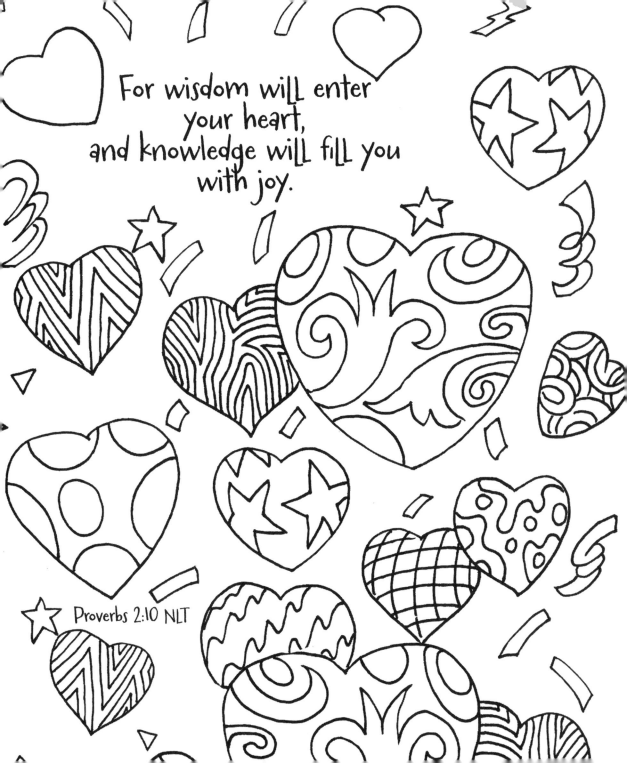

I WILL GIVE THANKS TO THE LORD WITH MY WHOLE HEART;
I WILL RECOUNT ALL OF YOUR WONDERFUL DEEDS.

PSALM 9:1 ESV

_____

_____

_____

_____

_____

_____

_____

_____

_____

_____

_____

_____

_____

_____

_____

_____

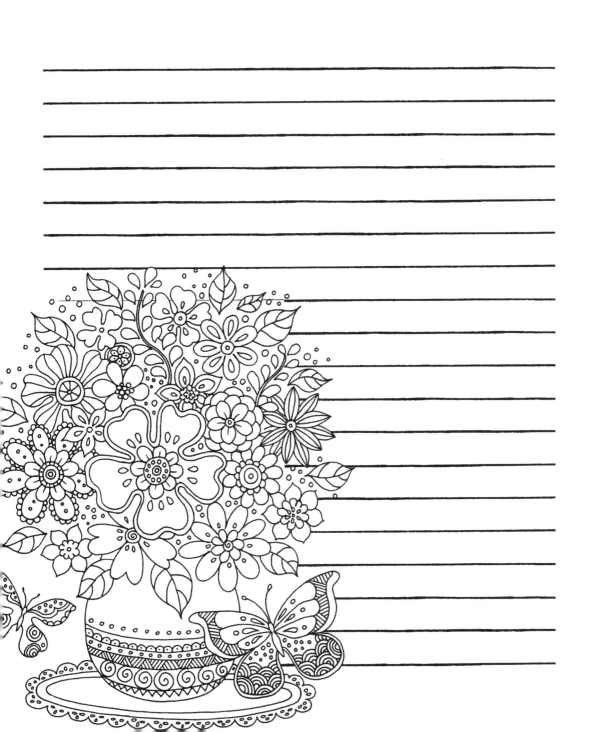

_____

_____

_____

_____

_____

_____

_____

_____

_____

_____

_____

_____

_____

_____

_____

_____

_____

REJOICE IN THE LORD ALWAYS. AGAIN I WILL SAY, REJOICE!

PHILIPPIANS 4:4 NKJV

I WILL BE GLAD AND EXULT IN YOU;
I WILL SING PRAISE TO YOUR NAME, O MOST HIGH.

PSALM 9:2 ESV

_____

_____

_____

_____

_____

_____

_____

_____

_____

_____

_____

_____

_____

_____

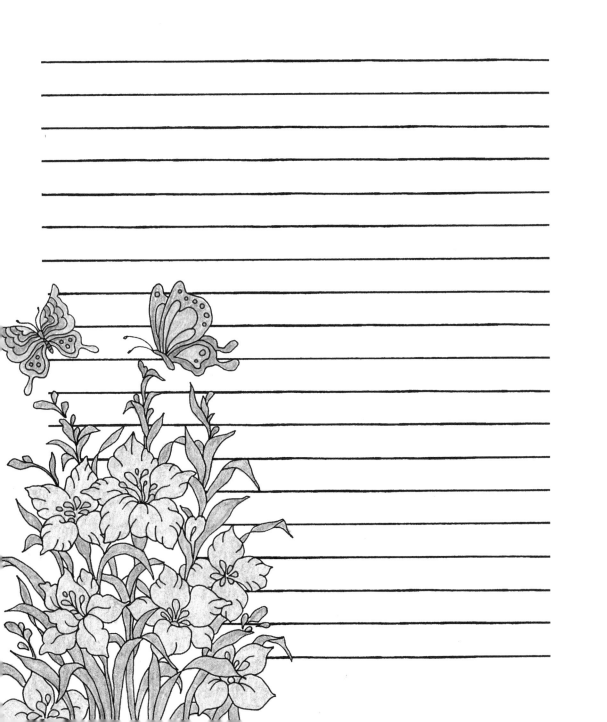

FOR THE LORD IS GOOD: HIS STEADFAST LOVE ENDURES FOREVER,
AND HIS FAITHFULNESS TO ALL GENERATIONS.

PSALM 100:5 NRSV

SATISFY US IN THE MORNING WITH YOUR UNFAILING LOVE,
THAT WE MAY SING FOR JOY AND BE GLAD ALL OUR DAYS.
PSALM 99:14 NIV

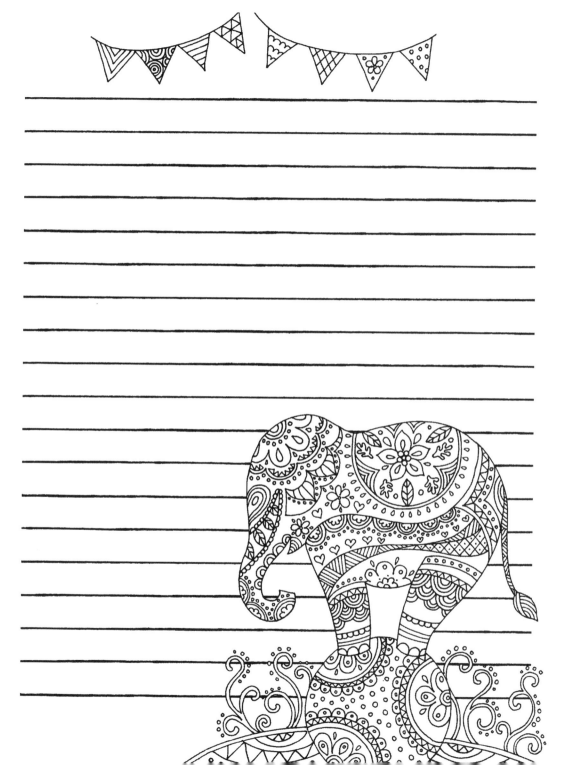

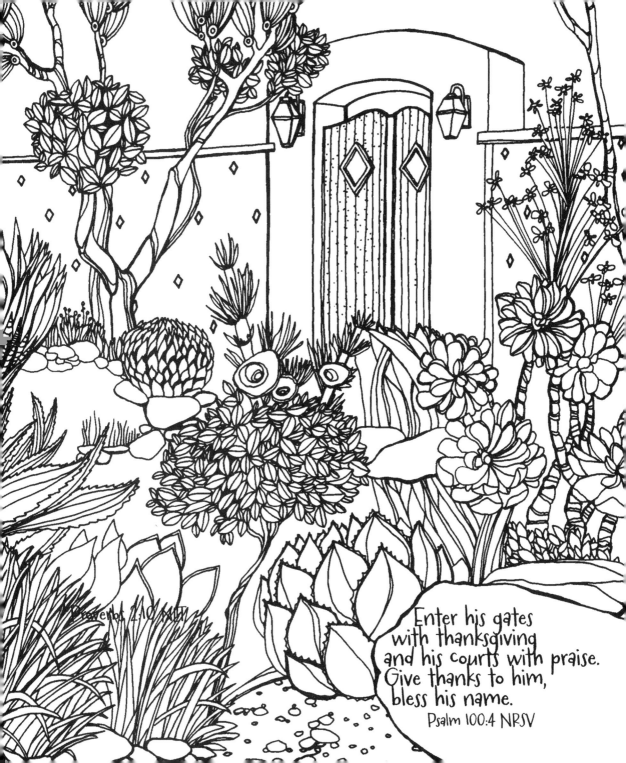

Proverbs 2:10 MEV

Enter his gates
with thanksgiving
and his courts with praise.
Give thanks to him,
bless his name.
Psalm 100:4 NRSV

LORD, HOW WONDERFULLY YOU BLESS THE RIGHTEOUS.
YOUR FAVOR WRAPS AROUND EACH ONE AND COVERS THEM
UNDER YOUR CANOPY OF KINDNESS AND JOY.

PSALM 5:12 TPT

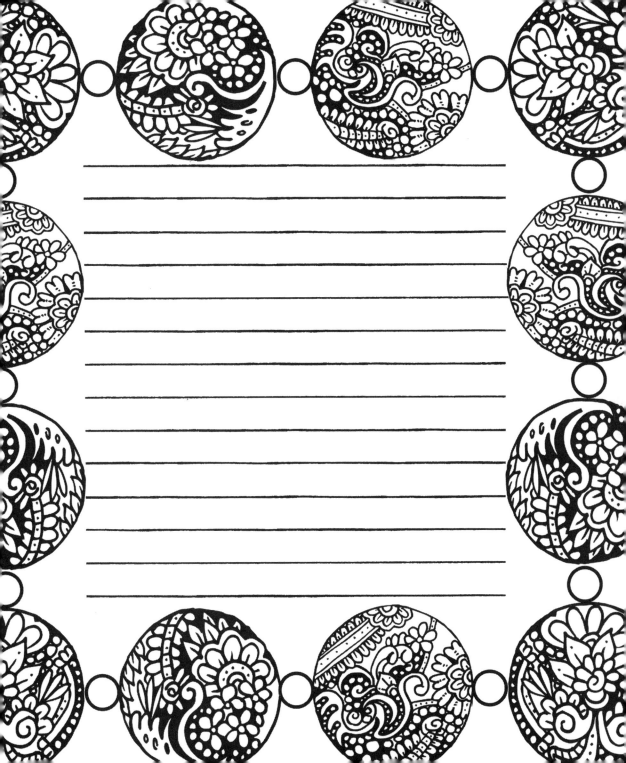

_____

_____

_____

_____

_____

_____

_____

_____

_____

_____

_____

_____

_____

_____

_____

_____

_____

LORD, I HAVE ALWAYS TRUSTED IN YOUR KINDNESS, SO ANSWER ME. I WILL
YET CELEBRATE WITH PASSION AND JOY WHEN YOUR SALVATION LIFTS ME UP.

PSALM 13:5 TPT

I WILL SING MY SONG OF JOY TO YOU, THE MOST HIGH,
FOR IN ALL OF THIS YOU HAVE STRENGTHENED MY SOUL.

PSALM 13:6 TPT

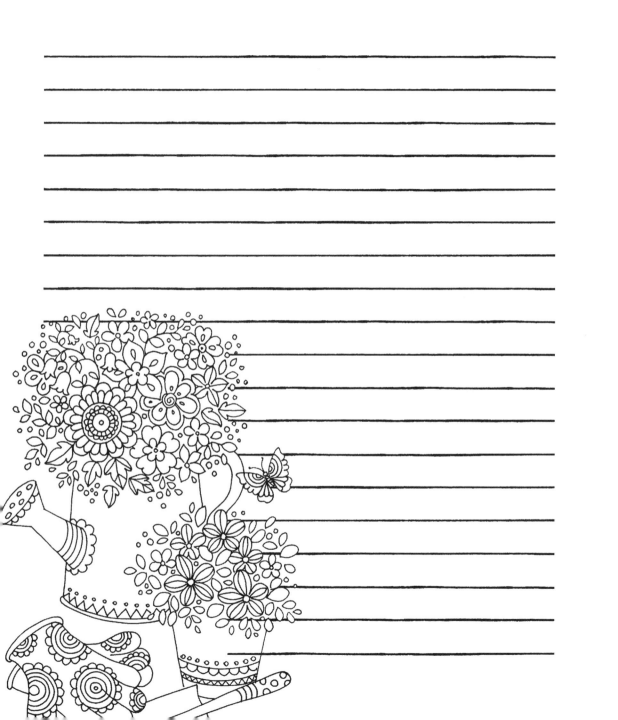

_____

_____

_____

_____

_____

_____

_____

_____

_____

_____

_____

_____

_____

_____

_____

_____

_____

MY HEART AND SOUL EXPLODE WITH JOY—FULL OF GLORY!
EVEN MY BODY WILL REST CONFIDENT AND SECURE.

PSALM 16:9 TPT

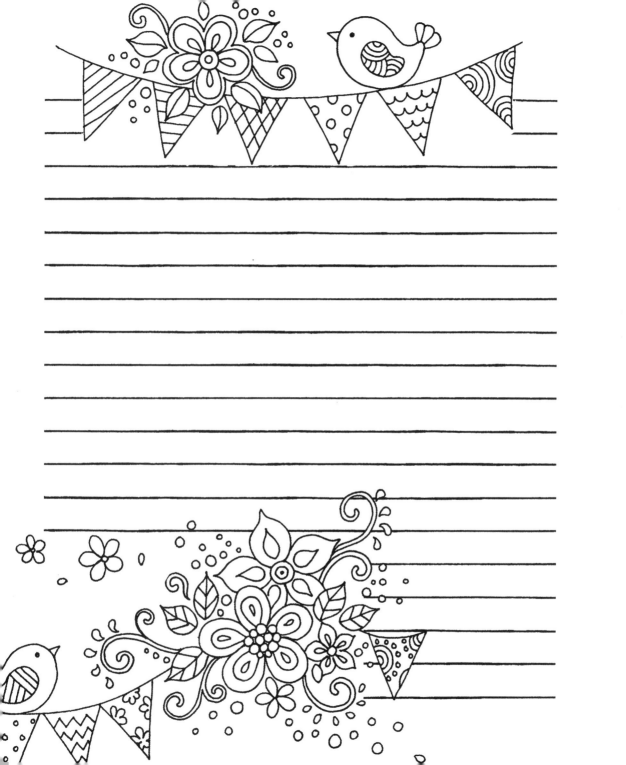

HIS TEACHINGS MAKE US JOYFUL AND RADIATE HIS LIGHT;
HIS PRECEPTS ARE SO PURE!

PSALM 19:8 TPT

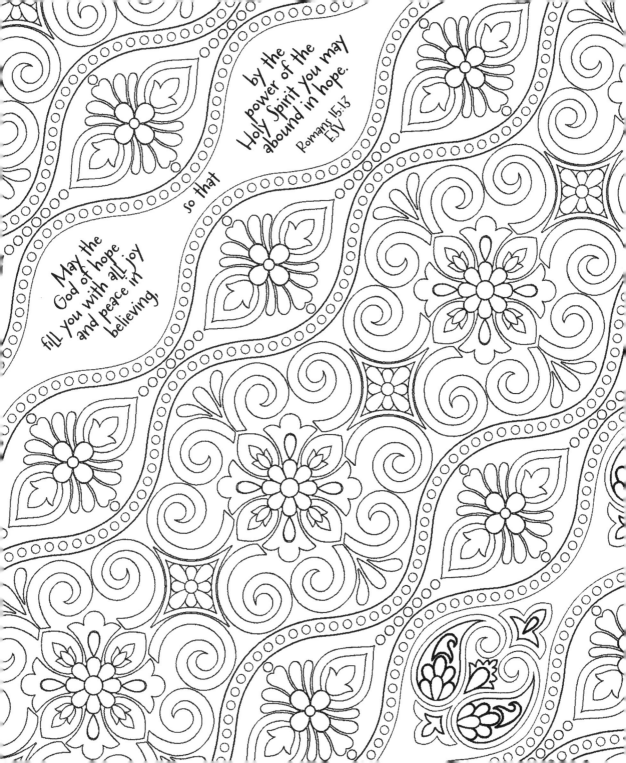

by the power of the Holy Spirit you may abound in hope. Romans 15:13 ESV

so that

May the God of hope fill you with all joy and peace in believing,

ALL WHO SEEK THE LORD WILL PRAISE HIM.
THEIR HEARTS WILL REJOICE WITH EVERLASTING JOY.

PSALM 22:26 NLT

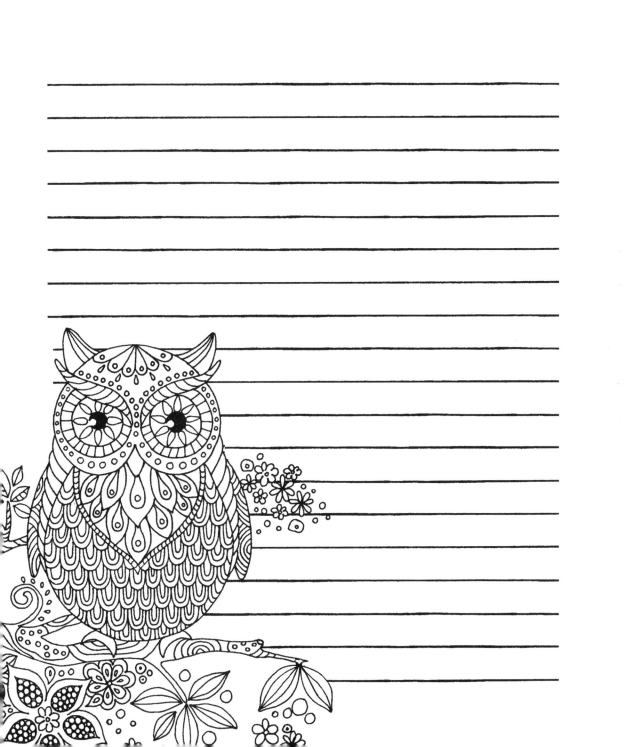

_____

_____

_____

_____

_____

_____

_____

_____

_____

_____

_____

_____

_____

_____

_____

_____

_____

AT HIS SANCTUARY I WILL OFFER SACRIFICES WITH SHOUTS OF JOY,
SINGING AND PRAISING THE LORD WITH MUSIC.

PSALM 27:6 NLT

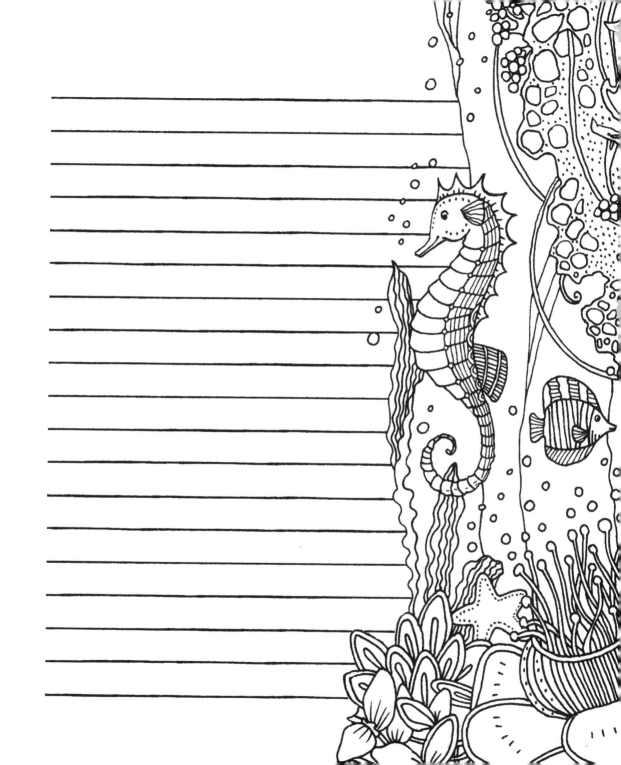

WHEN I FULLY TRUST IN YOU, HELP IS ON THE WAY.
I JUMP FOR JOY AND BURST FORTH WITH ECSTATIC, PASSIONATE PRAISE!
I WILL SING SONGS OF WHAT YOU MEAN TO ME!

PSALM 28:7 TPT

_____

_____

_____

_____

_____

_____

_____

_____

_____

_____

_____

_____

_____

_____

_____

_____

_____

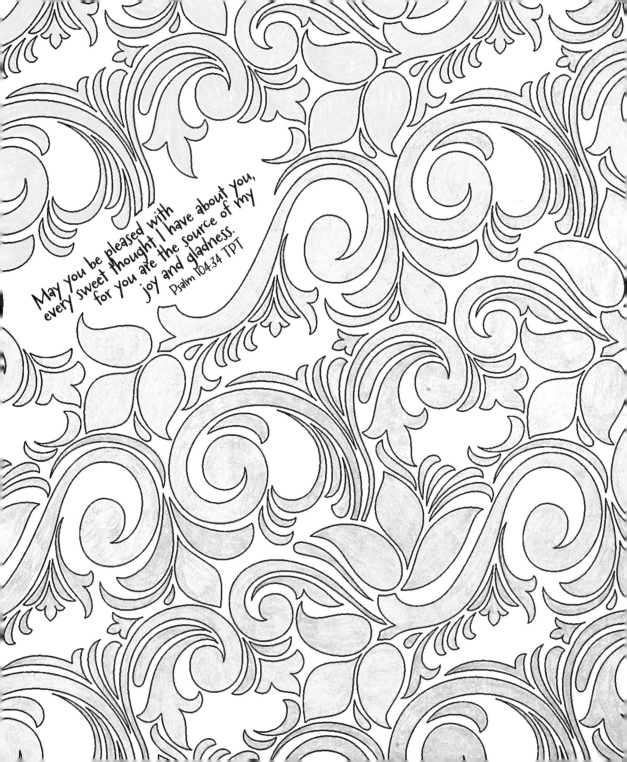

May you be pleased with every sweet thought I have about you, for you are the source of my joy and gladness.

Psalm 104:34 TPT

_____

_____

_____

_____

_____

_____

_____

_____

_____

_____

_____

_____

_____

_____

OUR HEART IS GLAD IN HIM, BECAUSE WE TRUST IN HIS HOLY NAME.

PSALM 33:21 NRSV

_____

_____

_____

_____

_____

_____

_____

_____

_____

_____

_____

_____

_____

_____

_____

_____

GAZE UPON HIM, JOIN YOUR LIFE WITH HIS, AND JOY WILL COME.

PSALM 34:5 TPT

I WILL REJOICE IN THE LORD: I WILL BE HAPPY WHEN HE SAVES ME.
PSALM 35:9 NCV

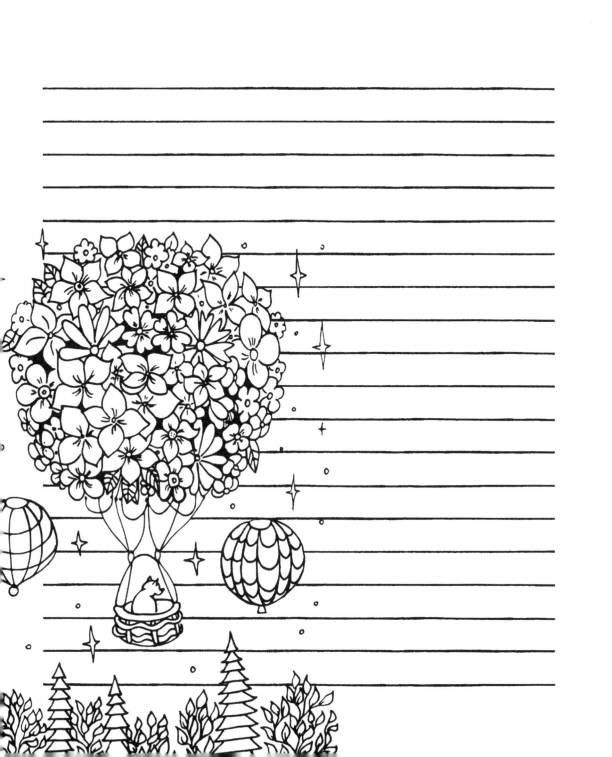

_____

_____

_____

_____

_____

_____

_____

_____

_____

_____

_____

_____

_____

_____

_____

_____

LET THOSE WHO FOLLOW YOU BE HAPPY AND GLAD.

PSALM 40:16 NCV

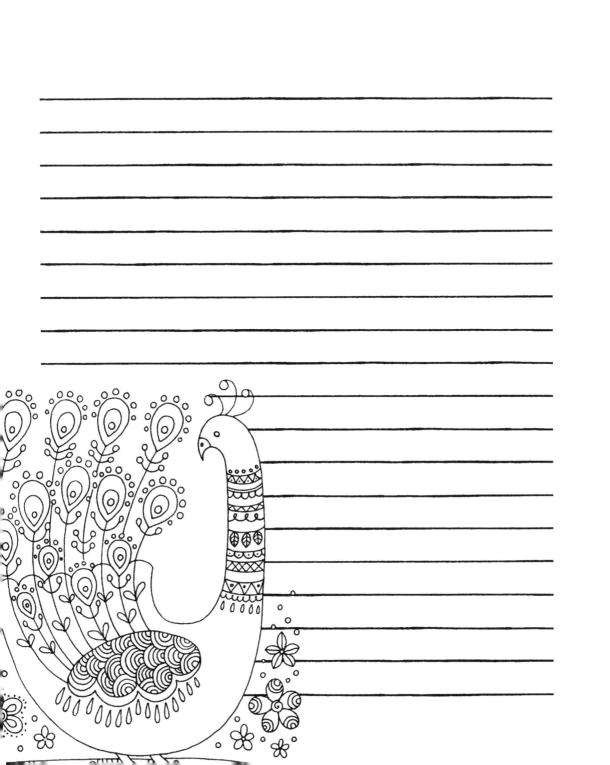

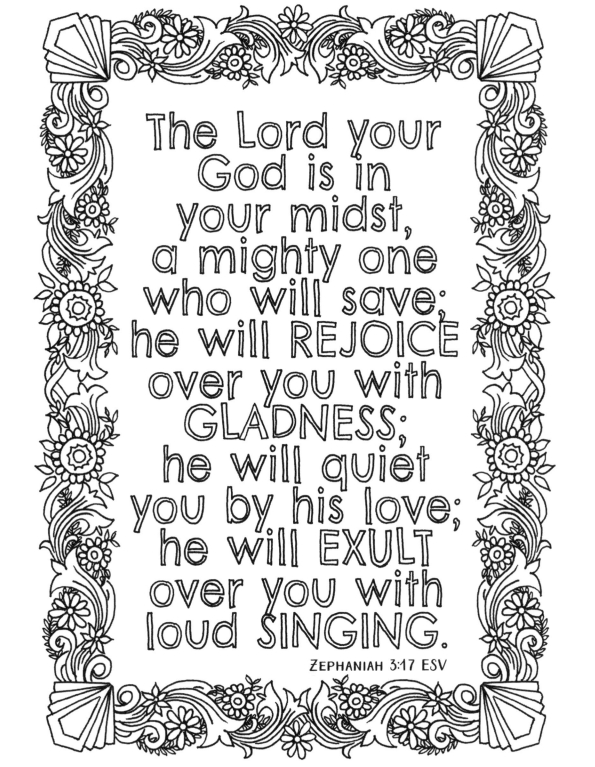

The Lord your God is in your midst, a mighty one who will save; he will REJOICE over you with GLADNESS; he will quiet you by his love; he will EXULT over you with loud SINGING.

ZEPHANIAH 3:17 ESV

GOD HAS A CONSTANTLY FLOWING RIVER WHOSE SPARKLING STREAMS
BRING JOY AND DELIGHT TO HIS PEOPLE!

PSALM 46:4 TPT

_____

_____

_____

_____

_____

_____

_____

_____

_____

_____

_____

_____

_____

_____

_____

_____

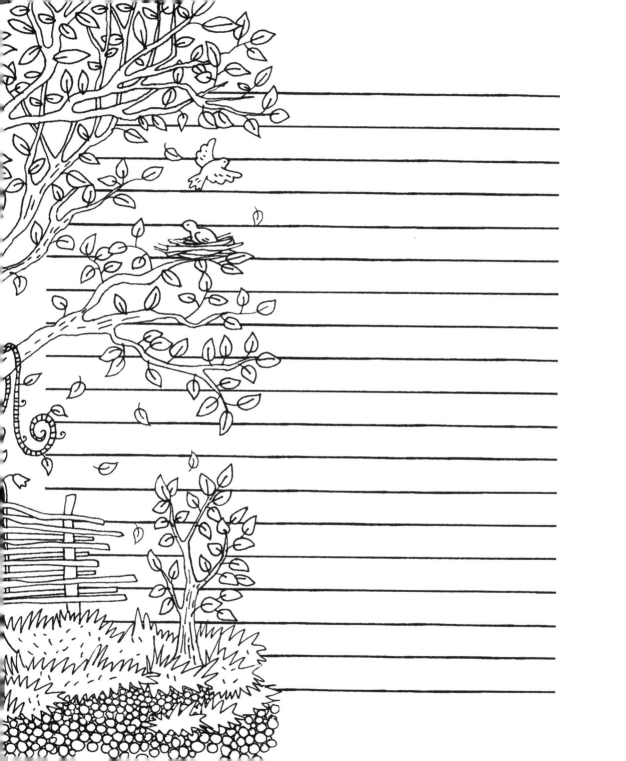

_____

_____

_____

_____

_____

_____

_____

_____

_____

_____

_____

_____

_____

_____

_____

SATISFY ME IN YOUR SWEETNESS, AND MY SONG OF JOY WILL RETURN.

PSALM 51:8 TPT

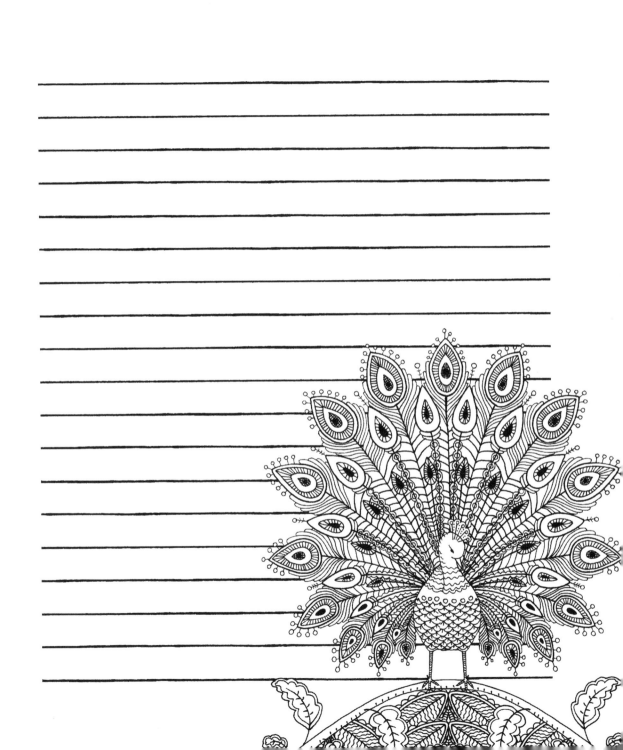

AS FOR ME, YOUR STRENGTH SHALL BE MY SONG OF JOY. AT EACH AND EVERY SUNRISE, MY LYRICS OF YOUR LOVE WILL FILL THE AIR!

PSALM 59:16 TPT